T0208382

ONE SOUL, MANY LIFETIMES

L. M. HENDERSON

Balboa Press books may be ordered through booksellers or by contacting:

Balboa Press
A Division of Hay House
1663 Liberty Drive
Bloomington, IN 47403
www.balboapress.com
1 (877) 407-4847

Print information available on the last page.

ISBN: 978-1-9822-3501-7 (sc)
ISBN: 978-1-9822-3502-4 (e)

Balboa Press rev. date: 09/16/2019

CONTENTS

INTRODUCTION

This book is intended to inform and not to try and make a believer out of the reader on the subject of reincarnation. If you do believe, it will enhance and reinforce your thoughts on the subject. If you don't believe and have an open mind, it will give you food for thought and ease your belief that we only live once, and that after death we don't exist. Nothing could be further from the truth on what happens after we leave this planet and go "home."

What a shame it would be if we only had one chance to live on this earth and accomplish everything we wanted and needed to do and then nothingness. When you think about it, it doesn't make much sense, does it? Even though we live longer in these modern times, it doesn't always allow us to finish what we set out to do and try to accomplish in one lifetime.

This book is about my experiences with spirit and my likes and dislikes and fears that were unexplainable to me until I looked into and read about reincarnation. I come from a family of believers and intuitive people that reinforced my beliefs and made me understand what was happening and why I felt a certain way about many aspects of my existence, including the people that graced my life along the way.

I know people who don't believe in an afterlife or reincarnation, and death is a scary word for them. It shouldn't be, and I'm writing this book to help those who fear this inevitable transition in their lives. I don't want to sway people one way or another, but to just give the reader another way of thinking of who we are and why we decided to come here in the first place.

I hope when you read this book you'll be entertained by it and also think about and contemplate what I'm saying to you from my heart and soul. The information in this book is meant to enlighten you and make you feel better about all the possibilities that exist in all of our lives. It's endless what we can accomplish in the many lifetimes that all of us have left to live in this world.

CHAPTER ONE

This book is a compilation of experiences and knowledge of reincarnation as seen through my eyes. There have been many incidences where I couldn't explain why certain things were happening or why I felt a certain way, such as fear or a strong feeling about something, until I began to read about reincarnation and listening to my grandmother and mother about their beliefs on this subject. Now it all makes sense. The idea that we live many lives to learn and evolve our souls answers many questions we all have about our existence. The following is one of the stories I'd like to share with you. I think you'll find it fascinating.

When I was only 5 or 6 six years old, I loved lying on the floor in our living room in the flat we lived in in San Francisco, and listen to my Mom's opera records. We had an old radio console and on top of the unit was a record player. The speaker was in the front, so I lay on the floor listening to what was playing. When I say opera, I mean the full production of Lucia di Lammermoor, or Lily Pons singing in her glorious coloratura voice from the opera Lakme and wishing that someday I could sing like that. I wore these records out listening to them.

Now, how many children do you know at 5 or 6 years of age that are interested at all in opera? I thought so. There was a reason I was compelled to listen and also why I took piano lessons at age 6. These lessons would later help me to accompany myself in practicing and learning the arias and songs I needed to learn. Later on in life, around the late 1960's, I was cast in the Sound of Music, and the woman who played Mother Abbess was a singing coach. I took lessons from her and wanted to learn musical comedy. However, she saw in me the potential to sing opera! I didn't believe her but she insisted. I practiced and practiced and eventually my voice was trained well enough for the opera stage.

The love of opera is in my soul and started when I was very young and also from two other lifetimes spent in Italy. Later on in this book I will explain a lot more about my love of opera and what I learned from a dear psychic friend who has crossed over now. I learned a great deal from my readings and will never forget her.

In learning about reincarnation you will find that the people in our lives are there for a reason. We all have lessons to learn and experiences to go through and these people we call friends or family are there to help us achieve this. We also help them. Nothing is by chance. People don't come into our lives by chance. We've all been through many lifetimes with these people in many different roles. Did you ever meet someone and felt like you knew them well? Did you ever meet someone and didn't want anything to do with them? This is soul memory. You've crossed paths before with these people. We've all experienced this, I'm sure.

Keep an open mind as you continue this journey with me. I think you'll be fascinated and will have many questions along the way.

CHAPTER TWO

Another chapter in my life involves water. Deep water. The fear of this has been so embedded in my soul and I'm happy to say I know why now. It took almost a lifetime to find out why I have this fear of deep water.

When I was very young, mom and dad would take me to the movies with them if the movie was appropriate for me. One of the movies I remember seeing was The Pearl. It was a story about a precious pearl in a giant clam on the bottom of the ocean. Men would dive to find it and of course it was a story about who would find it first. When they were under the ocean looking for the clam, I would be sitting in my seat in the theatre slowly rising up from my seat trying to get my breath! It was frightening and I felt like I was drowning! Yes, it was true. I did this without causing a fuss and my parents weren't even aware of what was going on. This happened every time we saw a movie that had anything to do with the ocean or other deep water.

My mother would wash my hair with me lying on my back in a tub of water and her arm supporting my neck. It was frightening to me. I would be crying and telling her to get me out of there. I didn't know and my poor mother didn't know why this was happening. It just was.

Later on in San Francisco mother took me to a community center to have swimming lessons. My parents finally realized how scared I was of the water. The lessons were a fiasco and didn't work. I would stay in the shallow end of the pool not enjoying myself at all. I wanted to get out of there.

I went through life not swimming and not caring about the water one bit. We never had a pool and I didn't belong to the YWCA or any other club that had a pool. If there was a pool nearby I would sun bathe and that's all.

When I was in high school the powers that be, would warn everyone that if we didn't pass the swimming test of swimming across the pool we wouldn't graduate. Imagine how I felt about that one! I knew I couldn't pass that test if my life depended on it. So here we are in the pool on this particular day, and everyone is passing the test but me. I was petrified of the deep end. There was a girl in the pool who was a very good swimmer and the swimming instructor asked her to help me across the pool by holding my hands all the way across.

We started at the shallow end and I was face down in the water with my eyes closed and she was holding my hands. She's pulling me across and all of a sudden I was grabbing onto her and she was trying to grab onto me and pull me the rest of the way across. I didn't realize what was happening. All I knew was that I was afraid and wanted to get out of there fast. When we got to the deep end of the pool, she looked at me and said that when we got to the deep water I automatically stopped moving and wouldn't budge. She was struggling to get me to move so she could get me to the end of the pool. I did all of this subconsciously. With my eyes closed I just knew we were at the deep of the pool and I wanted out.

I couldn't explain this, and no one else attempted to find out why I did this. Of course I graduated from high school. It was a scare tactic so people would try harder to swim across that pool. If I knew then what I know now about reincarnation, I would have had my answer as to why I was so petrified of deep water. As long as I'm on top of the water in a boat, I'm fine. I've taken countless cruises in my life, and I even took sailing lessons with my sister and thoroughly enjoyed it. However, I will admit, when my sister and I would go out far enough that the waves were getting higher, I said we should head back and end our sailing time.

In a later chapter I will explain the reason for all of my fears, talents, and other aspects of my life and also who I am. These experiences I'm telling you about in these earlier chapters are to let you know how I got to where I am today. You'll see how my life was transformed into finding out why I felt a certain way about things, the fears, likes and dislikes, and what I believe to be true today and how I'm comfortable with all that has happened in my lives.

CHAPTER THREE

Have you ever met someone in your life that you felt totally comfortable with and had no negative thoughts having to do with them? Thinking about them and being with them just comes naturally, doesn't it? This chapter is about how I met my late husband, Chuck, and how quick everything fell into place from beginning to end.

I had a four year relationship with a man I met in high school. He was from Germany and has since crossed over. I can't say that I loved him, but he was there to take me to the junior prom and the senior prom which at the time was very important to me. We had fun, but he was more serious about me than I was about him. We broke up in 1959, very shortly after my graduation from high school. I found a job at Crocker Bank in San Mateo and worked there about a year. I was lonely and looking for a boyfriend. I was seventeen years old. My mother got tired of me moping around the house and not going anywhere or doing anything productive.

One day she said to me, *why don't you go to Hillbarn Theatre and audition for a play or something?* Hillbarn was a very popular theatre group in San Mateo, California. It was in an old church with plenty of charm. I had never been there before to see a play or audition for one. Of course, I balked and said I didn't want to.

There were two one act plays going on at the theatre, and one night after work I went to see them. I checked the theatre out and got a feel for the place and decided I would audition for a play in the near future. I watched the plays, and the one called *Cold and Beautiful* interested me the most. Why? Because the male lead, Chuck, who would later become my husband, was handsome, interesting, and was a good actor. I came home and explained to mom and dad about this man I saw in the play. I said that he had thinning hair but was good looking. I had no idea if he was married or what he was like.

The theatre had set painting and construction days on the weekends. People came and volunteered their time to get the set ready for production. I went on this particular Saturday to help paint the set for the upcoming play. As I'm painting I noticed a man painting part of the set also, and realized it was Chuck who had been in the play I saw. I started up a conversation with him and told him how much I enjoyed his performance in the one act play. I looked at his *ring* finger and noticed a gold ring on it. I figured he was married. He was friendly and we kept painting and talking.

Later that same year, 1959, auditions were announced for a comedy entitled *The Warrior's Husband.* My dad came with me to the audition to make sure I was in a safe place, as parents do. The director asked me to read and also dad.

Dad said, *oh no I'm not interested in being in a play,* I came with my daughter and she wants to read. Needless to say, I got into the play and so did Chuck. Well, the rest is history for those of you who know me. For those who don't, Chuck and I got engaged before the play ended and were married the following June of 1960.

You're probably asking yourself what this has to do with reincarnation. Let me explain. I was a very shy human being as a child and into my teens. My boyfriend from high school was the only beau I had before getting married. I didn't date like other kids in school. When I met Chuck, I hardly knew him but something inside of me knew this man was it. It was hard to explain. He was familiar to me, and I knew in my heart he was the man for me in this life. You should have seen the other cast members in the theatre when we told them we were engaged! It was fast, it was a little scary, and it was right. We both knew it and it was *meant* to happen.

Each of us comes back to earth in different lifetimes to assume another role with the same souls we've been involved with before. We know these people this time around and can't explain how or why, but we just know. Sometimes it's a welcoming familiarity, and sometimes it isn't. It can work both ways. When it's not so good, I believe we're brought together to resolve whatever issues we have with that soul and move on. When it's good, everything falls into place beautifully. That's how meeting Chuck was for me. Beautiful!

I don't believe in coincidences. I know you've heard the expression, *everything happens for a reason.* I'm here to tell you it does! Everything was right about our marriage. We were married for 46 years before cancer took him. Neither of us ever regretted the fast courtship and marriage. We had two beautiful children early in our marriage and have loved and cherished them ever since. No regrets whatsoever.

My life changed completely when my beloved Mother said, *go to the auditions, and get out of the house.* Also, thank you mom! What was meant to be came into fruition.

Think back on your lives and ask yourself how certain things of importance that were life changing, happened without much explanation as to how they occurred. I'm sure you could come up with a few of these events in your lives. We all have a journey in our lives. We get there with help from our family, friends, and even strangers. I always call life a chess game. All the characters are in place for someone to make a move to change everything. When all the moves are done, and everything and everyone is in place, *checkmate!*

CHAPTER FOUR

Have you ever longed to visit a certain place on this Earth? To see it, take in the scenery and the food, and get to know the people? I have too. That place is Italy for me. When I studied opera and trained my voice, it was in the Italian language which I love. It's a romantic and beautiful one that flows off the tongue when speaking or singing it. I'm not fluent in Italian but I pronounce it correctly and the Italians can understand me when I speak to them in their language.

As I grew older I became more passionate about Italy. I've been there several times on cruises with my family and also alone. From Italy we have been blessed with gorgeous music, unbelievable art and sculpture, and the food is to die for. When I hear Italian opera, my heart melts with the beauty of it.

In September 2010, I went on a cruise to Italy by myself. It was incredible and I'll never forget it. When I go there it's like I'm going home, and when I leave it's like leaving that home. I can explain all this passion for Italy as you keep reading on.

Years ago I met a fellow opera singer in an opera I was cast in and we played two of the three cabaret singers who sang together throughout the opera. They were the comedy relief. I'll call my friend Annabelle, which isn't her real name. We got to know each other well. As years went by Annabelle became more psychic and intuitive and eventually it became part of her life's work. Years went by and I didn't know whatever happened to her.

One night I was watching an informative news program and they were showing interviews about various people in different walks of life. I was doing a crossword puzzle and wasn't paying that much attention to the program. Suddenly I heard the name *Annabelle*, and I looked up. They were interviewing her and explaining how she'd located a missing person in the exact spot where he was eventually found. I was dumbfounded. There she was. Talk about synchronicity!

I finally found her after a lot of inquiries and utilizing the internet. She lived in a town just south of me. I called her to make my first appointment for a reading. In all, I had seven readings from her and they were incredible and informative and they helped me a lot. Having psychic readings is a sort of therapy for me. When I lose someone I love, having a reading and being in contact with them through a medium is wonderful. It has helped me tremendously.

I asked about my trip to Italy which was in September as I stated in the previous paragraph. To back track a little to give you some history of how Annabelle conducted her readings, I want to mention that the late clairvoyant Edgar Cayce, known as the sleeping prophet, would show up during her readings to talk about a person's health and other issues. He was always there to help her with the readings. It was wonderful and I always had a great respect for him. I've read his books and he was amazing. He could read a person's body while asleep and tell them all about their health issues.

To continue with the reading, Cayce said that this trip to Italy will be very good for me. He said to let go and enjoy everything. I know I have lived in Italy twice before. Hence, my love for this place. The first lifetime there was in the 14th or 15th century. I was a male musician and played the concertina. My uncle had made a beautiful concertina for me that people used to admire. We had a trio and we'd sing and play. Cayce called it the "squeeze box." I played by ear and we'd perform in small theatres and musical plays. I would also write music.

I was entranced with this reading and it didn't end there. Around the 18th century I had lived in Milano and had sung in operas. My man friend at the time would stand backstage and listen to me sing and enjoyed it immensely. We lived in a beautiful home on a knoll where the breeze would blow through open windows.

I now understand completely why I love Italy so much. I have had at least two wonderful lives there in the past. In this reading Cayce also said that I would meet a person on this trip who would have a sense of recognition of me somehow. After the reading I forgot about that particular information. However, on my last tour before coming home, the tour guide was an older woman and it was a tour of a winery in Tuscany. Beautiful! It was the highlight of the trip.

As I was taking a picture of the lemons growing like weeds there, the tour guide came up to me and asked me if I was Roman. I said no, not in this lifetime. But I have lived lives in Italy before. She said that the lifetimes go by quickly. That was all that was said. But I remembered what Cayce had said and it gave me chills. The way she asked and the look on her face when I answered her convinced me that there was a moment of mutual recognition of who I was. Incredible!

In the next few chapters I will tell you more about readings that I've had with Annabelle. These readings have helped me understand who I am and why I have certain fears and likes and dislikes in my life. This information is invaluable.

CHAPTER FIVE

In another reading from Annabelle, I asked why I had such a feeling for the Native Americans. I love their spiritual philosophy and I feel what they went through in America and elsewhere. I love Native American art, and these things are a part of my life. What came through in this reading was amazing.

As I mentioned in Chapter Two about my fear of water, this reading will explain that fear and why I have it.

Apparently I was a Pawnee Indian girl, and my father was a chief. He had a headdress of white feathers. I was called "running water." I used to go by the river and fill a pail with water and bring it back. I never went into the river. One day a torrential flood hit the area and I drowned! It was very quick and we were totally caught unprepared. I was 15 or 16 when it happened.

To this day when I see anyone under water in a movie, my breathing becomes labored and I want them to get out of that water. These memory cells don't disappear. They affect our lives in many ways. If I were to learn to enjoy the water and not be afraid in this lifetime, I would have to be hypnotized. However, that probably wouldn't work because I like to be in control of my faculties at all times.

My love for Native American art and culture is a good thing. I'm happy having my house decorated with paintings, and other forms of art depicting the designs and culture of these very important people in our world. The only negative thing I carried over to this lifetime was the drowning and the fear of water to this day. Even with this fear, I took sailing lessons with my sister in the early eighties and loved it. Of course, she took care of the sails, and I manned the helm.

I also love to go sailing on big ships and travel to different places. I love the water when I'm on top of it and can look out at the horizon. I thoroughly enjoy this. I have the ship around me to protect me and that's a good thing!

Quite a few years ago my sister tried to teach me to back float in a beautiful pool at the residence of a friend at the time. She and I became frustrated! When I tried to lie on my back in the water I would sink. I couldn't keep my legs up and this only proved to me personally that the body can't float on the water when it's so thin and not a solid thing. Of course, that's not true but in *my* mind it is! This fear is pretty deep seeded, so I will continue cruising on big ships and having a great respect for the ocean and big bodies of water and appreciate their place on this earth. We need this water. I just don't need to swim in it.

CHAPTER SIX

For those people who know me, I don't like to discuss the world of politics. I stay away from them as much as I can. However, I don't know when it started or why, but I absolutely love studying the life of Abraham Lincoln. I like his philosophy and what he did for our nation. He was a remarkable man. I honor his memory by keeping a bust of Lincoln in my office along with some pictures taken of him in that era.

I have books about him and articles, and I'll explain this affinity I have for him in the next few paragraphs.

Quite a few years ago, two friends of my late husband and I got married in Sonoma. I had to find a B&B for my husband and I to stay in for the weekend. I went online and randomly chose one not knowing anything about it or the history. One morning after breakfast the owner of the B&B and my husband and I were the only ones left at the table. All of a sudden this woman said to me, *I have to tell you a story about this place.* I thought, okay that would be interesting. She proceeded to tell us about the original owner of the B&B and that he was a sculptor and how he was commissioned to do a bust of Lincoln which is now in the basement somewhere at the Smithsonian! I was dumbfounded, and my husband sat there quietly.

This woman knew nothing of my interest in Lincoln or why it was important for me to hear this. I never forgot it. There are forces at work all the time in our lives and beyond. Spirit plays an important role in our lives constantly. I randomly chose a B&B that had an important history of Abraham Lincoln whom I was so interested in and had so much memorabilia about his life and what he had to say.

At the 2010 reading from my psychic friend Annabelle, I asked why I had such an affinity for Lincoln. She explained this and I was astounded. Apparently in Lincoln's lifetime before his presidency and during his time of being our president, I lived two lives! He was present at this reading and he was smiling at me according to Annabelle. If only I could see as Annabelle did.

My first life was during the Civil War as a young man and I walked with Lincoln and listened intently to what he had to say because I was mesmerized by him and was in awe. We talked about how important the land was and how it gave us food to survive. Annabelle said I had a long rifle hanging from my waist which was almost bigger than I was. Apparently I died young during that time.

My other life at the time of Lincoln was as a slave in the south and it was during this time that he abolished slavery.

What I want to say here is, as spirits of the universe we need to experience all aspects of life, negative and positive, to advance our souls and gain knowledge. The lives that have left an impression on us and influenced who we are now, are the ones we have a slight remembrance of in this present lifetime. We have glimpses and dreams and circumstances that are hard to explain sometimes. My readings however have explained many of these feelings and they make sense to me now. These lifetimes I've shared with you in this book were important to me and influenced what I've accomplished in this lifetime. It was all explained to me beautifully.

One last thing before we end this chapter. During the reading regarding Lincoln, Annabelle related that Lincoln was sad because he wasn't finished on this earth. He had a dream about his assassination. Imagine if he were president today. I would relish that. We need the honesty and compassion for his fellow man that he had in his heart.

CHAPTER SEVEN

Many people believe that the life they're in right now is the only one they will have, and that after they're gone there will be nothing but blackness and nothingness. In other words, they will cease to exist in any form! That to me is a very scary thought if it were true. It would make no sense to live one life and then die and never to be heard from again. There's no purpose to it. This chapter will explain to the readers that the former scenario is not true. I feel it, I know it, and the things that have happened in my life proved to me that we exist even after our bodies die. There *is* life after death. In fact, I don't like to say we die. I say we cross over to another dimension, which is our home. We come from there on the other side and we return there after our lives here are finished.

Through the years I have had readings from many psychic mediums. I've gone with my mother when she was alive, I've gone with friends, and I've gone by myself. Some were okay, and some were extraordinary. When relatives came through and said something that only I knew, I considered that was for real. In other readings there was standard info that could come from anyone. One needs to be very aware of their reader and have full trust in them. If you have any doubts at your reading with a psychic, you need to seek another source. I've been pretty lucky finding some amazing psychic mediums.

Annabelle was the best. I'd known her for years and she had an extraordinary gift. Her psychic abilities improved over the years and became even stronger than when she started out. I had seven readings from her before she crossed over. Having readings was a kind of therapy for me. When I was going through a stressful time, when important decisions had to be made, or just to hear from those I loved that crossed over, I needed a reading. She gave me confidence to try and figure these things out for myself. I've learned to look inside and get the answers to questions that emerge from my mind.

During these readings from Annabelle, my late husband, my mother, and my grandmother would come through and leave me messages. It was exciting and reassuring to me that they were around and watched over me. Be reassured my readers, that whoever you loved and they have crossed over, they are looking out for you and are by your side. They have not disappeared. They have only gone home which on the other side is only three feet above us here on earth. They're with us always. Isn't that reassuring? Doesn't it make you feel good to know that you haven't lost your loved ones forever?

In one particular reading, Chuck, my late husband, came through and said that everything I told him when he was alive was true. He felt like a dunce! I answered, knowing Chuck would hear me, that we all know things at the right time and when it's necessary. He used to tease me about reincarnation and psychic info and readings that I had. He acted like he didn't believe and didn't want to know. Well, now he knows! The nonbelievers will know when they cross over. The believers know while they're here on earth through dreams, psychic happenings in their lives, and an innate knowledge that can't be dismissed. We all get this information when it's time! Having an open mind and letting this information come through helps a lot. It's a reassuring and safe feeling to know we don't end when we cross over.

In the next few paragraphs I want to share some of the visitations I had from my late husband, Chuck, after he crossed over. The scenario is that after someone close to us crosses over, they are around us for about a year to make sure we're okay and that things are coming along as they should. I was amazed by these visitations. They came to me in a dream state and were very real and not the usual feeling one has in a dream. He was definitely there. I think you'll be amazed also when you read this. My purpose in telling you is so that you will understand that we truly are watched over and loved by the people who have transitioned to the other side. The love never ends.

He was sitting on my right side about three feet above me. As I said before, the Other Side is about three feet above where we are here on Earth. He was wearing a plaid shirt, which he always wore. I touched his left arm and thanked him for letting me *feel* his presence.

If any of you have had the pleasure of seeing the movie *P.S. I love you*, there's a scene in the movie in which I totally identified with. It happened to me. I was in bed and felt someone get in with me in a *spoon position* and I was adjusting the sheets like my husband and I always did. I was in a *twilight* state and said "I can feel you." He said yes. It was an emphatic yes as if he accomplished this with some effort and was proud of himself. I couldn't open my eyes, and I've been in this state before. I woke up in a peaceful mood and in awe of what just happened. I'll never forget it. I cried when I saw this happen in the movie mentioned above.

There's a fabulous garden statuary place on Highway 92 here in Half Moon Bay that my husband and I always wanted to go to but never did. In 2007 just before Valentine's Day I was planning on going there. However, I was compelled to go there on February 14th and not before or after. When my gut talks to me, I listen. So I went on that day. What a wonderful place. They have fountains and statuary that are perfect for various types of gardens. I love elephants with a passion. Anyone who knows me knows this. I happened upon an elephant fountain that wasn't too big. Adorable. However, I had to look at other things before deciding. I couldn't put that fountain out of my mind. I went back to it and I bought it. As I was going to my car, the owner who was going to deliver it the next day to my home said, "happy Valentine's Day" to me. I was shocked. I didn't know him and immediately I knew it was Chuck who was responsible for the trip to this place and leading me to the elephant fountain. It was definitely a Valentine's Day gift from my beloved husband. I called the elephant *Ananda* which means happiness in Sanskrit.

Two days before what would have been our 47th anniversary, I sensed Chuck's presence. He and I were in a kitchen hugging, and I told him he makes me feel good. I thanked him for coming to me. He said "let's put on a play together." We met at a theatre group in 1960 and through our whole marriage of 46 years we were in plays and musicals together. It was a big part of our life. I told him in response that I was doing the best that I could here and that someday when I'm over there where he is, that we would perform together again.

A month after Chuck crossed over, I dreamed that we were driving somewhere and we made a stop. Somehow I got lost when we both went our separate ways for errands or something. Sometimes dreams are vague and we only remember the important things. I couldn't find Chuck and I asked someone where a certain building was and they couldn't tell me. I called him on the cell phone and he answered and I told him where I was. I could hear him walking towards me with his familiar shuffle. He came and got me and I hugged him and said "I knew you'd find me." He whispered in my left ear that he loved me, and I said I loved him.

It was almost a year since Chuck had crossed over. Mother, Chris (my sister), and I went on a cruise to Italy. I had vivid dreams on that trip. First, a little dog was barking in my dream while I was asleep and it startled me so much I sat up in bed a little shaken. I've never done that before. I went back to sleep and then I was dreaming that I was sitting at a table with my head down. Chuck was drinking a cup of coffee and I kissed his hand and then he rubbed the back of his right hand along my left cheek. I absolutely felt that gesture. The next day when I told my mother what had happened she said, "he was saying goodbye."

Ten years have passed since Chuck's crossing over, and I've had dreams of him now and again, but never with the realistic intensity that those visitations were in my life. I'll never forget them. It proved to me that we do go on after life here, and we do care and love those we've left behind, and that life on Earth is not the end. Our souls are forever. We are in transition always. Think of it as a trip and you go from one place to another and experience what there is in each of those places. That's how we evolve through eternity.

CHAPTER EIGHT

How many lifetimes we will have depend on where we are in the progression of our soul. Some souls try very hard when they're in a lifetime to experience everything around them, get involved in all things that are interesting to them, and to live as much of a rich and adventurous life as possible. Also, when people recognize their *given* talents and work on them and advance these talents to a satisfying development, they have accomplished an important step in the progression of their souls. The quantity of lives depends on the quality of lives we have lived. If you live life to the fullest and have many experiences either good or bad, you're fulfilling your soul's purpose and probably won't have to return as often. If you go through life having no interests, no ambition, no purpose or desire of any kind, you will definitely be coming back and improving on that scenario until you realize that you must fulfill your purpose in a particular lifetime.

We're not on this earth to just play around and do nothing. We have a purpose and each one of us needs to think deep and spiritually about why we're here. It could be any reason why you chose to come here. If you can't think about why, think about what you like. What touches your heart, what animals do you love, how do you react to music of any kind, does travel interest you? There are so many things to think about as to why you're here. Maybe in this life you're meant to give of yourself such as healing, helping those in need, traveling to other countries where poverty abounds. There are so many other reasons to live life to the fullest. I've only mentioned a few to stimulate your mind of all the possibilities for you to experience.

I like to use analogies when explaining something that can be hard to understand, especially for those people who haven't read about reincarnation before and are just now being introduced to it. Think of the many lifetimes that people lead as going to school here on earth. You go from kindergarten to your senior year in high school. With each grade you finish you get a report card, and also diplomas along the way. If you go on to college you get a degree with each set of courses you take. Your reward is that diploma or degree and then you're ready to get out in the world and find employment in the career you chose.

From your very first life here on earth, it was a learning experience and it was all new to you. One can't possibly accomplish what they need to do in one lifetime or even three or four. You have to go through the learning experience as you did in school. With each lifetime you live on this earth you are progressing a grade further in the learning process. Just as in school. After many lifetimes and learning experiences, you get the final reward. That is, you won't have to come back to earth for any more lifetimes and you can live in peace, beauty, and serenity with other souls at home on the other side. We know that as heaven. When we go *home* we are progressing and work to help other souls.

This is our reward because there is no physical pain, no diseases, no hate, no war, just loving souls and love of all kinds. We all long for this peace, but we have to come here to earth to evolve our souls and experiences before we're ready to live in heaven. Deep inside ourselves we know what's coming when we leave this earth. However, we have a contract with our maker to fulfill when we come here. If we don't accomplish the things we need to do under this contract, we come back again and again until we get it right. It's that simple. It really isn't rocket science. You don't have to physically see all of this to believe in it, just look inside yourself and meditate if you're not doing it already. Meditation allows you to reach inside where your soul and spirit lives and benefit from the thoughts and feelings you get from doing this. It relieves stress, and inspires you to receive thoughts and ideas that you wouldn't normally get in a busy and frantic world.

As long as you live on earth you're going to have stress and impossible situations. How you handle these things is how your soul develops and understands what to do to get out of those scenarios that cause disharmony with life around you. If one doesn't know how to handle negative situations, they get in deeper and just fret and sometimes cause physical ills in the process. Nothing that happens on this earth is as important as harmony within yourself and your love of other people in your life. When you have love in your heart and soul it can help solve many problems and situations. Remember, don't sweat and fret the small stuff, because it's *all* small!! Nothing is worth ruining your life for, and though it seems impossible at the time, just inhale deeply, close your eyes, and think of the possibilities of how to get out of a situation or make one better. Getting angry doesn't solve anything. It only can make things worse. Be the mediator and peacemaker and you'll feel so much better for it.

CHAPTER NINE

In this chapter I want to talk about forgiveness. Every one of us at one time or another has said something or done something to hurt another human being. They could be our dearest friends, family, and even a stranger. Most of the time we didn't mean what we've said or done, and wish that we could take it back. We've all been there, right? Also, most of the time we forgive those that hurt us, because the one that hurt you is sorry for what they've said or done. It sounds easy doesn't it? Forgive and forget. Well, let's talk about those that hold grudges and will *never* forgive those that hurt them. What a waste of energy, health, life, and time, to feel this way. Think about it. The stress of holding grudges affects the health in ways you can't imagine. Also, every time you see this person or hear their name it brings up old hurts. Why? Why do people let a remark or action eat away at them for the rest of their lives? It's not worth it. Believe me. To be free of this negative reaction to a remark or action is wonderful.

Forgive and forget. This also involves past lives. You're asking yourself right now, how? Let's say you knew someone in one of your past lives and you didn't get along at all. You were foes and hurt each other in ways that left an impression on your soul. Then, you find yourselves in this present lifetime together again. How do you know this? Okay, here it goes. You meet someone either at a social function or even in your own family and immediately you don't like that person. This person also has issues with *you*. The problem here is neither one of you know why in this lifetime you feel that way. Our souls have cell memory. Whatever trauma happened in a past lifetime is still in your deep thoughts. It's like we're given a little hint of that past experience in order to make it right in this lifetime. It's wrong for people to carry on and on feeling negative with a past hurt in this lifetime or another lifetime.

In all of our lifetimes we have met people that we immediately liked, and also those we didn't like. We don't always know why this happens. It's been my personal experience that sometimes I don't care for someone I've met and each time I see them I still feel the same way. Then, for some reason, as I get to know them better, I end up liking them. We may have been enemies in another lifetime but we were meant to resolve it in this lifetime. It's a great feeling when that happens. After all, whatever someone did to you in another life, no matter how horrible, is gone and done with and they are reborn in this lifetime to make amends. They basically aren't the same person. You can't condemn a person for what they've done to you in another incarnation. We grow, we change, and we're all trying to live out our lives as best as we can.

Forgive and forget. Start anew and make this lifetime the best life you can. You'll feel physically better, mentally clear, and enjoy the people around you and live a productive and peaceful life. Don't hold grudges because those feelings will eat away at you. They truly will. Friends and family are very important in your life. Without them you're lonely and have no one to turn to when you need them. This kind of love is unconditional. Experience it and find out what forgiveness really is.

CHAPTER TEN

In this chapter I'm bringing up another scenario of how we live different lives and experience different things. It's called "parallel lives." Some of you are thinking, *now what is she saying?* When I talk about these things I'm using my experiences in life, my gut feelings, and what I feel I know in my heart and soul of what's happening in our lives. We are very busy souls in our journey through these lifetimes. We are constantly on the move and constantly interacting with other souls to evolve where we need to be.

Wherever you are now in this lifetime, pieces of your soul which are pure energy are somewhere else on a different plane of existence living another life with other souls. What? Yes, I know it sounds unbelievable to some of you, others not so much. In other words, on this earth this isn't your only life that's going on! It took a while for me to believe this and understand it. I do though, and it's fascinating. You've all experienced Déjà vu, right? You've also met people that you swear you've known before, and also people you wish you didn't know. These familiar feelings could either be you're experiencing these feelings on a parallel life or you actually did go through these things in another lifetime through reincarnation.

We are not meant to know every lifetime we've led or *are* leading in another dimension. It would literally drive us crazy with all that information. Only once in a while do we get a glimpse or feeling of something or someone very familiar, and only when we need to know this to help in our present existence. It's meant to help us and keep us on a steady voyage in this present life. All of these existences and experiences interact with each other in various ways. Most of us write it off as a coincidence or strange phenomena. Not so true. I don't believe in coincidences. Everything happens for a reason. We may not know at the time why it's happening but it's for our own good and growth.

I have two short stories to tell you to explain about parallel existence. Before I tell you, I want to say that I truly believe in reincarnation, coming back in another body in another lifetime, and I truly believe in parallel lives. To me, they both exist. Of course, when we cross over we will truly know for sure exactly how we experience different lifetimes. I've read books in the past about both scenarios and they both make sense to me. We all need to have an open mind about it and take away the information that rings true. If you don't believe in certain things you have that right. If what you read here or anywhere else makes sense to you and you do believe it, that's a good thing also. Whatever happens in your lifetime, good or bad, you need to have an open mind and do the best you can to move forward. A lot of answers come through meditation and quiet time so you can think about things without interference. Go within yourself more than you do and tap that energy inside of you and you'll be surprised the thoughts you get and the answers you come up with without much effort. Now for those two stories I wanted to tell you.

When my husband Chuck was diagnosed with liver cancer he had six months to think about his life and recall it with thankfulness and love. He was one that never remembered his dreams. Once in a great while he'd remember bits and pieces. I on the other hand, remember many of my dreams. Even ones I had years ago. I get messages with my dreams and I've learned to understand symbolism and interpret them very well. He never understood how I could remember them. He said he never dreamed. Well, we all dream. If we didn't, we'd have mental problems and be a completely different person. Dreams are meant to heal and release stress.

We were having breakfast one day, and he looked at me with a serious expression on his face. He said he had a dream and remembered it and wanted to tell me. He wanted me to figure it out for him. I stopped what I was eating and was shocked that he remembered his dream. This is what it was. He was with a woman with blonde hair and a small child. He didn't know if it was a family of his or what, and the little girl wanted to come with him when he left. She wanted to join him where he was going. He said to her that it wasn't possible and she had to stay.

My jaw dropped open. He said it was crazy, and it probably didn't mean anything. He just remembered it vividly. I immediately thought about parallel lives and suggested to him that he had another life somewhere on another dimension. Of course, as usual Chuck looked at me as if I was crazy and brushed it off as weird! He never liked to talk about spiritual things and unusual phenomena because it bothered him. He didn't understand it and didn't want to deal with it. However, as I mentioned before in a previous chapter, after he crossed over he realized that all I was saying to him was true and he felt like a dunce. He didn't need to feel that way. We all find these things out when we're supposed to. He was getting close to death and there was a reason he dreamt about that situation. A lot of things come to light when we're getting near the time that our present lives are ending.

The other story I wanted to tell you is about my reading (in person) with Sylvia Browne in 2011. I have read a number of her books and learned a great deal about our past lives through them. She was a wonderful writer and as you read her books you feel like you're having a conversation with her.

During our reading, she told me that she and I help people come to earth for another incarnation. I asked her, "You mean you and I help these people?" I couldn't believe at first that Sylvia Browne and I helped people come back to this earth. She said she tells them not to go! Of course we laughed about that one and also agreed. My point in telling you this is while both of us were living a life on this earth at that time, our soul was also doing other things. In other words, we were living parallel lives! How else could I be sitting in her office getting a reading, and at the *same* time helping people incarnate? Wouldn't it be interesting to have a bird's eye view of our soul living various lives in other dimensions and realizing all the experiences we're having at the same time? It's mind boggling to try and analyze this scenario and truly understand it completely. The best way to deal with it is to think of our souls as a massive energy able to be anywhere and do anything it wants. Our bodies can't be in two places at the same time (as we often say!), but our souls can! Who we are is not just skin and bones. We are so much more and are very complex entities.

CHAPTER ELEVEN

We aren't given a handbook on how to live and how to bring up children. We just need to go by gut feelings and instinct. Hopefully we all have been taught what's right and wrong in our childhood. Unfortunately, some children haven't been given this lesson in life. They have to find out on their own and in the process make mistakes and bad decisions that affect them and the people around them.

Living on this planet is difficult with all the negativity around us. We must work very hard to ignore and repel this negativity and always envision the white light of peace and love around those we love and this earth we live on. The energy we surround ourselves with and others must be positive in order to carry on with our lives and to make decisions in the best possible and safest way.

Of course I get angry as you do when I see the news and read about killings and bombings and the mayhem going on in other countries and in the United States. It's normal to react to this, but after the initial reaction you must get back into the positive mode and share your energy and light to try and remedy the situation. You're probably saying to yourself, how can one person do this? You're right, not one person can accomplish this positivity, but if we *all* do this with sincerity on a regular basis it will work. Negativity attracts negativity, just as positivity attracts positivity. Which would you like to have in your life? I thought so.

I love being around people who are positive and fun and who laugh a lot. In turn, I do the same thing. I laugh about a lot of stuff that goes on in my life. Of course I don't laugh at the horrors that can happen in this world. I pray and send out positive thoughts. I believe that what we give out in terms of kindness and caring for people we get the same in return. Our actions and our words *really* do make a difference in our lives. When I'm in a quiet and funky mood and I'm out and about, I don't have a particularly pleasant day. Things bother me more and I feel like I should just go home! However, when I'm in a good mood, I smile at strangers and sometimes start up a conversation with someone and have a great day. None of this is anyone else's fault, it's mine alone. It's what I'm giving out that particular day

Each one of us has a spirit and a soul. I'll do my best to describe each one and make it easier for you to understand what they actually are. It has taken some time to figure this out and to differentiate the two. One needs to acknowledge their spirit and believe they have one. This spirit energy is actually part of God. A little piece of our maker is within all of us. It helps us function and make decisions in our lives. It ignites our souls to accomplish what we set out to do, and it is there to protect us and comfort us when needed.

I compare spirit to the spark plugs in a car. Without spark plugs the car won't work! Without letting our spirit work for us *we* don't work. Many people don't acknowledge their spirit and don't believe we have one. Of course, we all have to understand where we come from to feel this spirit within us. We all come from a higher power and no matter what religion or belief you have, we all come from the same place and our spirits function the same way. We need this energy to carry on as human beings. We can accomplish miracles and enjoy life when we realize who we really are at our core.

Our souls are the essence of our bodies and who we are as human beings. It is a replica of our bodies in a mirror image. Some people can see souls after they cross over. Many people call them spirits but they are actually souls that lived on this earth and who *still* live on the other side minus bodies. Our souls carry our thoughts and feelings that we had while living on earth. We also take the love with us that we felt when we crossed over. That does not die when our bodies cease to exist. Never.

After my husband crossed over, one night I came home late and was about to turn the light on in the laundry room and I saw a shadowed outline of my husband's body walk across the hall in front of me. I was startled but also was happy that it had happened. I haven't seen him since. However, I know he's around all the time. I feel his presence and he's in my dreams quite often. He's pure energy now just like everyone else who crosses over. We don't disappear into oblivion when we die. The essence of who we are is an eternal thing we possess. We all are unique in our personalities and thoughts and no one or nothing can take that away from us.

What shapes us into who we are is our upbringing, environment, people we know, our other lives before this present one, and other subtle factors. It explains our fears, phobias, likes and dislikes, our talents, and how we view life in general. There are so many ways this could go in people's lives. If there's too much negativity, you can get out of it. You need to try. It's for your benefit and for those around you. If there's positivity, you can use it to better your life and soar with your accomplishments. We are the masters of our lives. No one else can live our life for us. We are it. No excuses about what happened to you when you were a child, or that this happened or that happened. You can recognize it and do something about it.

CHAPTER TWELVE

Many people have had Near Death Experiences (NDEs). I'm not one of them. I have read many stories about people who have experienced them. They all share the same scenario when it is explained. They see a bright light, they feel peaceful, they see their life passing before their eyes, and have the feeling of wanting to go on and not come back to earth. The other side is truly our "real" home, and our time on earth is a learning experience and a time to atone for past negativities and relationships. Earth is not our permanent home. This may be hard for some to understand, but to read some of the stories of people who have crossed over and returned, it makes it easier to comprehend. They want to stay there in the peaceful, painless, and heavenly environment rather than come back to earth. The good news is, we *all* come from the same place, and we all return to the same place. We will eventually experience this heavenly existence when our time is done on earth, not before. We have a job to do here on earth and when that is finished, we will return home.

We all have numerous guides to help us on this difficult journey. It's not easy to ignore the negativity on this earth, and we have to work hard to create a positive environment to counteract it. We have difficult decisions to make in our lives, and that is where our guides help us. Never be afraid or hesitant to ask for their help when you need it. I always do. This helps me to make the right choice when the time comes. Yes, sometimes we make mistakes but that happens when we don't think things through and we don't ask for the help when we need it. Our guides and loved ones that have crossed over help us when we ask for it.

Life after death on this earth is not total blackness and nothingness. Unfortunately, some people believe that there is only darkness when we leave this planet. I'm here to tell you that it's *not* true. How do I know? Besides the feeling in my gut, I have an inner knowing that we are very much alive as pure energy when we leave our bodies. Memories of our lives are as clear as a bell. Think about it. When you dream and carry on with whatever you're doing, it's basically the same as when we cross over. When you are still in the body, you wake up and the dream is a little vague. We don't disappear! Who we are stays alive through eternity. We only come back to earth when we need to change our way of thinking, thereby atoning for our past mistakes. We evolve through this incarnation.

On the other side, we help souls to come back to earth. Conversely, we also help them to go home. Many souls teach while on the other side, and we're always busy giving of ourselves. This pure energy that we are when we leave our bodies enables us to go anywhere, do just about anything, and to revel in the knowledge that we are more aware of things around us than when we were in body form. We are powerful beings, and that spark of God, which is our spirit, is even stronger when we leave here to go home. How we live our lives here on earth, determines how we live our lives at *home.* The more compassion, love, and understanding we learn here on earth, carries over to our lives after we cross over. You never lose it, it goes with you. It's up to you how you want to live your life. Isn't the feeling of love more satisfying than hate? Don't you feel good when you've helped someone? Don't you feel good when you've helped a needy animal? Doesn't it feel good to give rather than take?

The purpose in living other lives is to learn and improve ourselves and our way of thinking and acting. We all need improving! None of us are perfect. It's true that we don't remember our other lives consciously, but there are little hints occasionally that come through that portion of our brains that we have no explanation for except a possible slight remembrance of times past. Use this knowledge that comes to you, let it help you through this life you're going through. It comes to you for a reason. In fact, live by this thought, that nothing is accidental. *Everything* happens for a reason. You have certain strong likes and dislikes, right? Some things frighten you and other things thrill you. You've had that feeling that you've been here before, and have done that before. These are the little hints that you have no explanation for in your everyday life. Use these slight remembrances to help you. They come to you for a reason. Recognize them and do whatever you have to do to make life easier while you're here.

CHAPTER THIRTEEN

As I write this last chapter, I'm devastated by the wildfires, the warming of Alaska, the melting glaciers which have an impact on our oceans, our lives, and wildlife. I pray hard that we can survive the eventual devastating impact this climate change has on all of us living on this planet. The climate is changing all over the Earth. I believe a lot of this change is us and our use of destructive materials we use that changes the delicate balance of this beautiful ecological wonder. These are the things that are hard to not take to heart as it's happening. I strongly believe that we should not take on all of the world's problems and worry about them every hour of every day. We can't fix every problem that arises. I never watch the news on TV before going to bed. Unfortunately bad news makes the news. They not only tell us what's happening, they keep at it for hours sometimes and our brains are saturated with the negativity of the incident.

We all need to be aware of what's happening in our world and around us, but once you know the situation, that's it. We don't need to harp on the negative aspects of it. We can pray for those affected but we have to go on with our lives. We're here to learn, and bad things happen all the time. We need to take a deep breath and go on living the best lives we can and overcome any kind of devastation.

Many people blame their present circumstances and their situation in life to past problems in their childhood or even past lives. Whatever happened to you in the past is just that, the past! Learn from those experiences, work past it, and make your life the best experience you can. Don't blame people in your past, family, friends, or foes, for how you live today and why you do certain things and react to certain situations. Remember, you can't *change* the past, the future isn't even here yet, and the only thing you should be concerned about is the power of *now*! Today, right this minute, what are you thinking, what are you doing to better your life and others, and what will you learn today that will help you through this life in the future? Do not constantly remember the bad things that happened in your life. To reiterate what I said in Chapter Nine, do not hold grudges against people in your past or present that have said things to you or have done things to you that hurt or have made you mad. You can't take words back. You can't change the situation that happened. Get past it, make up if you can, apologize, and move on with your life. Maybe your parents weren't the most understanding and attentive and you blame your misfortunes in your life on them. This is *your* life now and you can make it as positive and wonderful as you want. No one is to blame for your ills but you! Again, get past what other people have said and done to you. Love and positivity attracts the same thing in your life. If you are a negative person, you attract negativity in your life. It can't help but happen. We have the power to rise above past ills and misfortunes in our lives. Blaming negativity on past experiences is just an excuse for your actions. Be the best person you can be and guide your own life with positive actions and love that fill your heart. You'll be a much happier person for it. Believe me, I know.

Even past lifetimes can have a negative or positive reaction in how we live today. We are here to rise above it and carry on with this life as best as we can. Our past lifetimes are in our core memory and little memories pop up once in awhile to remind us of who we are. Certain fears, likes and dislikes, things you love and don't know the reason, are snippets of memory that crop up when needed. We need to get past our fears in this lifetime if possible. We also need to get past certain souls that were foes in another lifetime for whatever reason. We've met people in our lives that we have an instant dislike for and don't know why. We've also met people that we love instantly and don't know why. All these things are aids for helping us to get past the negativity that is holding us back from moving forward in this lifetime. Remembering these things also helps us to love even more than we do.

The main thing I want you to take from this book is love. These words were written with love. We're all in the same boat on this earth and want to find the easiest and most positive attitude towards life as we can get. There's so much negativity around us. We really have to fight to not let this infuse itself into our positive lives. This time around, we need to advance our souls in the way we think, the way we treat others, and to enhance our knowledge about life and why we're here.

I want to impress upon you that those who have left us and have gone home to the other side are *always* around us. They help us when we need it (I can attest to that!). They comfort us when we feel their loss or when we are upset. They never leave our side. These wonderful souls are pure energy and are able to be in multiple places at the same time. Our souls and who we are never die. Only our bodies get old and deteriorate and leave, not the essence of who we are. It's comforting to know this and I have had numerous experiences in my life to pass this knowledge on to you without hesitation.

Again, for the nonbeliever I hope this book has enlightened you and has caused you to think about reincarnation. For the believer, I hope this book has reinforced your belief in reincarnation. Eventually, we'll all know the entire truth when we cross over. For now however, I hope these thoughts, ideas, and experiences that I've shared with you, will bring comfort to your soul. Peace comes from within and so does our wellbeing and how we live our lives to the fullest. One of the most important things to think about is how we treat others. Each day do something to help others. I call it the ARK for the day, an *act of random kindness.* It can be big or little. It makes one feel good to be kind and help others. Don't you notice that feeling when you've done something for someone? I do.

Know that this life you're living now is not your last, unless you've totally fulfilled your reasons for being here. We all have souls that are evolving. Some have evolved to where they don't have to return to earth unless they want to. Others have to return because they realize they have more lessons to learn and they need to work them out in the next lifetime. We've all done this and no one is exempt. Know that no one dies, we cross over! We don't go away into dark oblivion. We reunite with our loved ones and we learn lessons at *home* as well as here on earth. We're always evolving and existing. Isn't this comforting? It's meant to be.

Please live a more positive life and enjoy it. Don't take the worlds problems on your shoulders and make your life miserable because of them. The problems in the rest of the world will be resolved eventually. Remember, this is a learning planet we are on. How we respond and resolve our own problems helps our souls to progress and be stronger.

When we are done with this life we are living, we cross over to a peaceful, positive, and enlightened place where our loved ones are waiting for us. I remember my late husband saying to me in a reading I had shortly after he crossed over: *When the trumpets blow, I'll come running!* I'm sure your loved ones will do the same thing.

Bless you all

Linda

Printed in the United States
By Bookmasters